The Christmas
Puzzle and Activity Book

ARCTURUS

ARCTURUS

This edition published in 2013 by Arcturus Publishing Limited
26/27 Bickels Yard, 151–153 Bermondsey Street,
London SE1 3HA

Copyright © 2013 Arcturus Publishing Limited

ISBN: 978-1-78212-218-0
CH002629EN
Supplier 13, Date 0713, Print run 2437

Colour and design by Dynamo Limited
Edited by Annabel Stones

Printed in China

This book belongs to

_____

_____

_____

CONTENTS

TOY STORY!

Here are two identical pictures of a toy store... or are they? There are six differences between the two. Can you spot them all?

STOCKING SEARCH!

This Christmas stocking has lots of different shapes on it.
Can you spot a shape that appears only once in one colour?

CHRISTMAS POTION!

Red and green are the colours of the season. So why not shake up some exciting drinks in these festive colours?

Here's what you will need:

★ CRANBERRY JUICE ★ GREEN FOOD COLOURING OR MINT EXTRACT ★ JUG OF WATER
★ ICE CUBE TRAYS ★ WHOLE CRANBERRIES ★ MINT LEAVES

Here's how to do it

1

Pour cranberry juice in a large punch bowl and place in the refrigerator.

2

Add a few drops of green food colouring or mint extract to the jug of water and pour into the ice cube trays. Place in the freezer until frozen.

3

Pour the cooled cranberry juice into clear glasses until they are three-quarters full.

4

Add some whole cranberries and mint leaves.

5

Shake the green ice cubes out of the tray and add to the juice.

6

Your fruity, festive drink is ready to serve. Enjoy!

WORDS WORK!

How good are you at guessing Christmas words?
Unscramble the letters using the picture clues to help you,
and then fill the words in!

1. LUBABE

_ _ _ _ _ _

2. TAFES

_ _ _ _ _

3. CRAFS

_ _ _ _ _

4. REDSPEHH

_ _ _ _ _ _ _ _

5. GESLIH

_ _ _ _ _ _

STAR ATTRACTION!

Just follow these simple instructions and add a sparkle to your room with your very own star!

Here's what you will need:

TWO SHEETS OF CARDBOARD ★ SCISSORS ★ FELT-TIP PENS OR CRAYONS
★ GLITTER GLUE AND SHINY STICKERS ★ A PENCIL

Here's how to do it

1

Draw a large star shape on one of the sheets of cardboard with the pencil. Cut it out carefully with scissors.

2

On the other sheet of cardboard, draw around the star you've just cut out. Then cut out this second star. Decorate both sides of the stars with crayons or felt-tip pens. You could also use glitter glue and shiny stickers to make your stars twinkle.

3

Cut a slit at the bottom of one star to about halfway up and then do the same to the top of the other star.

4

Slot the stars together by slipping one into the slit of the other. Now you have your own star attraction! You can make lots of different ones and hang them up with ribbon to make magical 3D decorations.

CANDLE CLUTTER!

This shining candle has lots of different shapes on it.
Can you spot a shape that appears only once in one colour?

TOY TREAT!

Look carefully at the order of the three toys below. Can you find them in exactly the same order in the box? Search from left to right, top to bottom and from the bottom upwards!

PRESENT PERFECT!

Here are two identical pictures of children on Christmas morning. Or are they? There are six differences between the two. Can you spot them all?

DING DONG!

Look at the list of words which are all to do with Christmas and find them in the bell.

★ Cheer
★ Carols
★ Santa
★ North Pole
★ Reindeer
★ Gifts
★ Elf
★ Stocking

MISSING BERRIES!

These berries should be attached to the wreaths!
Untangle the strings to see which bunch of berries belongs
to each wreath.

A   **B**   **C**

SANTA'S SECRET!

Decode the secret message that Santa has given to his elf and reindeer. Each letter should be replaced by the one immediately before it in the alphabet. For example, 'M' will replace 'N', 'A' will replace 'B' and so on.

N B L F   T V S F

X F   D B O   G M Z

I J H I   B O E   B M M

O J H I U   M P O H

LOADING UP!

Let's make Christmas colourful! Use paint, pencils or crayons to colour in the picture using the number key as a guide.

1 - Red
2 - Yellow
3 - Light Blue
4 - Light Green
5 - Black
6 - Pink
7 - Dark Blue
8 - Light Brown
9 - Dark Brown
10 - Orange

RACE-A-SLEIGH!

Here's a game that will have you racing on your hands! Get ready for some fast action as teams set the pace of the sleigh race.

Number of Players FOUR OR MORE (AN EVEN NUMBER) PLUS AN ADULT TO SUPERVISE THE GAME

Materials Required ★ STONES OR STICKS FOR MARKING OUT LINES

★ WHISTLE (OPTIONAL)

Object of the Game TO FINISH THE RACE AS A PAIR, WITH ONE OF YOU SUPPORTING THE OTHER BY THE LEGS AS HE OR SHE CRAWLS FORWARD USING ONLY THEIR ARMS.

1 On grass or a soft surface, use a stone or a stick to mark out the start and finish lines 10 metres (30 feet) apart from each other.

2 Divide everyone up into pairs and line up along the start line.

3 One player from each pair gets down on their hands and knees.

4 When the supervising adult calls out 'on your marks, get set, go!' or signals the start by blowing a whistle, pick up your partner's legs. Hold them by the ankles at waist height as you try to push the 'sleigh' (your partner) towards the finishing line.

5 Remember, broken sleighs must be picked up where they collapsed - they cannot walk to the finish line!

6 The first pair to cross the finish line is the winner!

You and your friends will end up with really mucky hands in this game! Don't forget to wash them afterwards!

BUSY SANTA!

Look carefully at the picture then try answering questions
on the next page. The sharper your memory is, the more answers
you will have. Don't be tempted to turn the page for a quick peek!

QUESTIONS

1. What is looking in the window?

2. What is Santa doing?

3. What is hanging on the wall?

4. Is there a ball in the room?

5. Where is the rocking horse?

6. Is Santa sitting down?

7. What are the elves looking at?

8. Is there a Christmas tree in the room?

GIFTS GALORE!

These gifts are all muddled up!
Can you count how many there are?
Lots of them overlap so count carefully!

PiCK OF THE PACK!

Here are six handsome reindeer. But one is not the same as the others. Try to spot the odd one out!

PLUM PUDDING!

What's Christmas without cake? Here's a recipe to make a mouth-watering winter plum cake!

Here's what you will need

★ 115G (4OZ) BUTTER ★ 2 EGGS ★ 1 TABLESPOON OF BAKING POWDER
★ 1/4 TEASPOON CINNAMON ★ 170G (6OZ) SUGAR ★ 110G (4OZ) PLAIN FLOUR
★ 1 TEASPOON ALMOND EXTRACT ★ 4 PLUMS, SLICED

 ## Here's how to do it

1 Start by preheating the oven to 175°C /350°F (gas mark 4) and greasing a 25 cm (10") cake tin.*

2  Put the butter and two thirds of the sugar into a bowl and beat it until fluffy. Add the eggs and almond extract. Sift the flour and baking powder together and add to the mixture in the bowl. Mix together with a wooden spoon.

3  Pour this batter into the cake tin. Arrange the plum slices on the top of the mixture.

4 Mix the rest of the sugar and the cinnamon together and sprinkle over the top of the cake. Ask an adult to help you place the cake in the preheated oven. Bake for 45 minutes.

5 After 45 minutes, take the cake out of the oven and leave it on the worktop to cool.* Enjoy your plum cake while it's still warm!

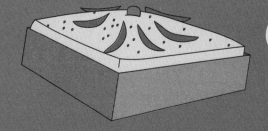

* Ask an adult to help you with this

WORD SCRAMBLE!

How good are you at guessing Christmas words?
Unscramble the letters using the picture clues to help
you, and then fill the words in!

1. KELWANFOS

_ _ _ _ _ _ _ _ _

2. PEELARCIF

_ _ _ _ _ _ _ _ _

3. RANGEM

_ _ _ _ _ _

4. YITAVNIT

_ _ _ _ _ _ _ _

5. THLIGS

_ _ _ _ _ _

SNOWFLAKE GREETING!

Every snowflake is unique, so why not make some snowflake Christmas cards to give to your friends and family? Follow these simple instructions and create special cards for everyone!

Here's what you will need

★ SQUARE SHEET OF WHITE PAPER ★ SCISSORS ★ GLITTER ★ GLUE ★ THIN COLOURED CARD

 Here's how to do it

1 Lay the white paper in front of you with the corners at the top and bottom. Fold the paper in half, from bottom to top - so that the folded edge is at the bottom. Take the bottom left corner and fold it to the top point. Then do the same with the right hand side. You will have a diamond shape.

2 Hold the bottom point and use scissors to cut an arc from the left point to the right point. When you unfold the paper, you will have a circle shape.

3 Fold your paper circle in half, then again, and again so that you have a triangle. Cut out shapes from the folded edges very carefully with scissors.

4 Open it out and look at your unique snowflake! Use glitter and glue to make your snowflake shimmer. When it's dry, stick the snowflake to a sheet of folded coloured card and write your Christmas message inside.

GiNGER JOY!

This tasty gingerbread man has lots of different iced shapes on him. Can you spot a shape that appears only once in one colour?

SMILE A WHILE!

Look carefully at the order of the three smiling faces below. How many times can you find them in exactly the same order in the box? Search from left to right, top to bottom and from the bottom upwards!

RUDOLPH REPLICA!

Here are two identical pictures of Rudolph and two friends... or are they? There are six differences between the two. Can you spot them all?

SNOWMAN MAKEOVER!

Look at the list of words all to do with snowmen,
then find them all in the puzzle.

★ Snowman

★ Carrot

★ Top hat

★ Charcoal

★ Twigs

```
          T M O C
      C R R A C R T
      G C A R R O T G
      A U C G T O W O
      M G M M C M I C
      G C U M C U G S
        O F L U M S
      C G F M G R C
    C L F L T O P H A T
  L T G C E G A P A R O
  R U P A R E C T R O T O
P R U N E S R O C C R C
R S N P S O R C O A T
  N C S N O W M A N A
    S C A C N O L M
        N O R M
```

STAR BRIGHT!

Look at the star at the top of the Christmas tree! Correctly trace the path from the very top to the bottom of the tree.

JUMBLE JAM!

Here's a list that will confuse Santa! Can you unscramble
the letters and rearrange them into words?

1. S R S H C T I A M   E R T E

_ _ _ _ _ _ _ _   _ _ _ _

2. C R D O E T A O S N I

_ _ _ _ _ _ _ _ _ _

3. S E E V L

_ _ _ _ _

4. C E B D E E R M

_ _ _ _ _ _ _ _

5. C E P N R A R

_ _ _ _ _ _ _

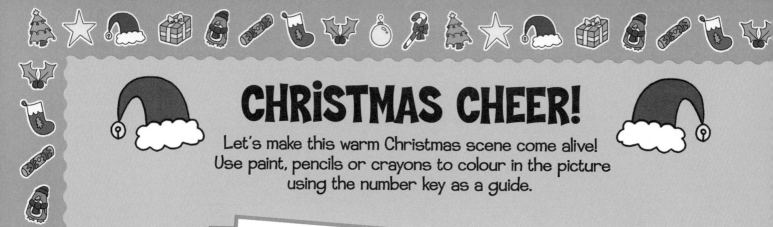

CHRISTMAS CHEER!

Let's make this warm Christmas scene come alive!
Use paint, pencils or crayons to colour in the picture
using the number key as a guide.

1 - Red

2 - Yellow

3 - Black

4 - Pink

5 - Green

6 - Brown

7 - Light Brown

8 - Blue

9 - Orange

PIN THE TAIL!

Here's a reindeer without a tail!
Can you pin a tail to it blindfolded?

Number of Players FOUR OR MORE, PLUS ADULTS TO
SUPERVISE THE GAME AND SPIN THE BLINDFOLDED PLAYERS.

Materials Required ★ A LARGE SHEET OF CARDBOARD ★ SHEETS OF PLAIN PAPER
★ DRAWING PINS ★ PENS ★ A BLINDFOLD ★ SCISSORS

Object of the Game TO CORRECTLY PIN THE TAIL ON RUDOLPH WHILE BLINDFOLDED.

1 Choose a playing area with plenty of room to move around in.

2 Ask an adult to help you draw a large picture of Rudolph on the sheet of cardboard. Hang it up on a wall at eye level.

3 Cut out as many paper reindeer tails as there are players. Insert a drawing pin in each tail. Be careful holding them!

4 Each player writes his or her initials on the tail they are given.

5 Take turns to blindfolded each player and spin them around three times and and then point them in the direction of the drawing. Make sure they don't get too dizzy and fall over!

6 After spinning around, walk towards the wall and stick the tail to the place you think Rudolph's tail would be.

7 The player who comes closest to pinning the tail in the right place on Rudolph is the winner!

Use your memory to picture Rudolph in your head before you spin round!

SANTA ON THE ROOF!

Here are two identical pictures of Santa climbing down the chimney... or are they? There are six differences between the two. Can you spot them all?

MAKING A SNOWMAN!

Look carefully at the picture then try answering questions on the next page. The sharper your memory is, the more answers you will have. Don't be tempted to turn the page for a quick peek!

QUESTIONS

1. How many children are there?

2. Is the snowman wearing a scarf?

3. Are the children wearing hats?

4. What animal is next to the little trailer?

5. What is the father putting on the snowman?

6. What is behind the trees?

7. How many trees can you see?

8. How many buttons do you see on the snowman?

SHOCKING STOCKINGS!

Everyone is looking for their stockings to hang up but they're all in a mess! Can you count how many there are in this picture?

SANTA SEARCH!

Here are six well-dressed Santas. But one is not dressed the same as the others. Try to spot the odd one out!

CHOCOLATE TREATS!

Christmas just isn't Christmas without little chocolates to snack on. So just follow this recipe and make some for you and your friends to enjoy.

Here's what you will need

★ 115G (4OZ) BUTTER ★ 170G (6OZ) SUGAR ★ 340G (12OZ) CHOCOLATE CHIPS
★ 170G (6OZ) CHOPPED WALNUTS ★ 340G (12OZ) COLOURED MINI MARSHMALLOWS
★ 200G (7OZ) DESSICATED COCONUT ★ 5 SHEETS OF WAXED PAPER EACH ABOUT 23 CM SQUARE

Here's how to do it

1  Ask an adult to help you fill 3/4 of a large saucepan with hot water and place it over a low heat. Put the butter, sugar and chocolate chips in a glass mixing bowl and place it in the saucepan.

2 Stir occasionally until the butter and chocolate melt into a smooth paste. Remove from heat and allow the mixture to cool.

3  Add the marshmallows and nuts to the chocolate mixture.

4 While the chocolate mixture is cooling, lay the sheets of wax paper on a flat surface. Sprinkle coconut on the wax paper.

5  Spoon a generous amount of the chocolate mixture on to the wax sheets. Roll up into a log shape. Leave them in the fridge overnight.

6 Take it out the next morning and cut into chunky slices. Peel off the wax paper and hey presto! A mouth-watering chocolate treat complete with a snowy winter covering!

TALKiNG PiCTURES!

How good are you at guessing Christmas words?
Unscramble the letters using the picture clues to help
you, and then fill the words in!

1. NICEM IPE

_ _ _ _ _   _ _ _

2. CHRUCH

_ _ _ _ _ _

3. DUNDGIP

_ _ _ _ _ _ _

4. FIGT

_ _ _ _

5. LAROC

_ _ _ _ _

EASY-PEASY BOWS!

These beautiful bows are really easy to make.
Stick them on your wrapped gift boxes to
make them impossible to resist!

Here's what you will need

★ A LONG PIECE OF RIBBON ★ A STAPLER ★ SEQUINS OR BEADS ★ GLUE

Here's how to do it

1

Take one end of the ribbon and make a small loop with it. The size of the loop depends on how big or small you want your bow to be.

2

Tightly hold the place where the end meets the main strip of the ribbon. This is called a pinch.

3
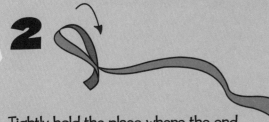

Still holding on to the pinch, take another short length of the ribbon (equal to the one you took earlier). Make another loop and pinch again.

4 Following a circular course, keep repeating the loop and pinch technique until your ribbon has at least six to eight loops (the more you make, the prettier your bow will look). Make sure you are holding the bow in the centre.

5
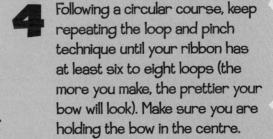
Staple the centre where the ribbon overlaps to secure the loops. You can staple twice so your bow is firmly in place.

6 Carefully apply some glue over the ribbon and stick a few tiny sequins or beads to cover it. When it's dry, your bow is ready to decorate your presents!

RING THE BELL!

This shining bell has lots of different shapes in it. Can you spot a shape that appears only once in one colour?

SANTA SEQUENCE!

Look carefully at the order of the three Santas.
Can you find them in exactly the same order in the box? Search
from left to right, top to bottom and from the bottom upwards!

DOUBLE TROUBLE!

Here are two identical pictures of a snowman...
or are they? There are six differences between the two.
Can you spot them all?

PRESENT PUZZLE!

Look at the list of exciting Christmas presents.
Find them all inside the beautifully wrapped gift box!

C	C	T	O	Y	S	P	C	O	A	O	W	C	A
O	E	W	T	T	W	P	H	W	C	W	A	A	C
M	O	M	B	E	S	A	O	S	W	C	E	M	A
P	P	E	T	S	A	S	C	W	E	L	A	E	M
U	A	R	B	H	W	H	O	R	T	O	H	R	T
T	S	B	H	O	O	A	L	O	R	T	R	A	R
E	R	O	A	E	W	L	A	T	L	H	E	S	M
R	W	O	A	S	R	E	T	S	R	E	H	A	S
S	R	K	H	W	K	H	E	O	O	S	E	R	T
E	K	S	T	A	E	M	S	E	W	H	R	H	R
W	R	I	S	T	W	A	T	C	H	E	S	H	H
E	C	W	I	T	A	W	R	W	T	W	R	S	E
W	C	A	R	D	S	A	C	T	H	W	H	R	S
R	W	E	D	L	B	I	C	Y	C	L	E	R	Y

★ Bicycle   ★ Computers   ★ Chocolates

★ Books   ★ Wristwatches   ★ Cards

★ Clothes   ★ Cameras   ★ Shoes

★ Toys   ★ Pets

RIDE A BIKE!

Poor little Billy! He got a bicycle for Christmas but can't remember where he has left it! Help him find it by travelling through this maze.

READY FOR CHRISTMAS!

Let's make Santa's sack colourful! Use paint, pencils or crayons to colour in the picture using the number key as a guide.

1 - Red

2 - Yellow

3 - Light Green

4 - Black

5 - Pink

6 - Dark Blue

7 - Dark Green

8 - Light Brown

9 - Dark Brown

10 - Orange

COOKIE CRUNCH!

How many cookies can you eat? You will need to eat the most to win this crazy stomach-filling game!

Number of Players SIX OR MORE.

Materials Required ★ TWO STOOLS ★ A PAIR OF CLEAN WASHING-UP GLOVES ★ A PLATE OF COOKIES ★ A DICE ★ A NAPKIN ★ A KNIFE AND FORK

Object of the Game TO TRY TO EAT AS MANY COOKIES AS YOU CAN BEFORE THE NEXT PLAYER'S TURN. IF YOU EAT THE LAST PIECE OF COOKIE, YOU WIN!

1 Place the two stools side by side. On one stool put the plate with the cookies; put the napkin and gloves on the second stool.

2 Players sit around the two stools in a circle. The youngest player is the first to have a go.

3 When it is your turn, roll the dice in front of the other players. If you get a number from 1-5 do not move. If you get a 6, rush over to the second stool, tie the napkin around your neck, pull on the gloves and start to eat the cookies with the knife and fork.

4 Remember, you cannot tuck in unless the napkin is tied around your neck and the gloves are on. Otherwise you lose your turn.

5 If another player rolls a 6, he or she will rush over to you. Remove the gloves and napkin as quickly as you can.

6 Players take it in turns to roll the dice. As soon as someone throws a 6, it's their turn with the cookies.

7 When you are out, take up your place in the circle once more. The player who finishes the last cookie is the winner!

CHRISTMAS VISIT!

Look carefully at the picture then try answering questions on the next page. The sharper your memory is, the more answers you will have. Don't be tempted to turn the page for a quick peek!

QUESTIONS

1. What are the children doing?

2. Is there a star on the Christmas tree?

3. What food is on the table?

4. How many baubles are on the tree?

5. Is there a guitar in the sack of presents?

6. How many children are seen in the picture?

7. Where are the holly decorations?

8. How many teddy bears are there on the floor?

SHOPPING SPREE!

Wow! That's a lot of Christmas shopping.
Can you count all the shopping bags in this picture?
There are lots that overlap so count carefully!

WHiCH GiFT?

These gift bags are bursting with exciting presents!
But one is not the same as the others.
Try to spot the odd one out!

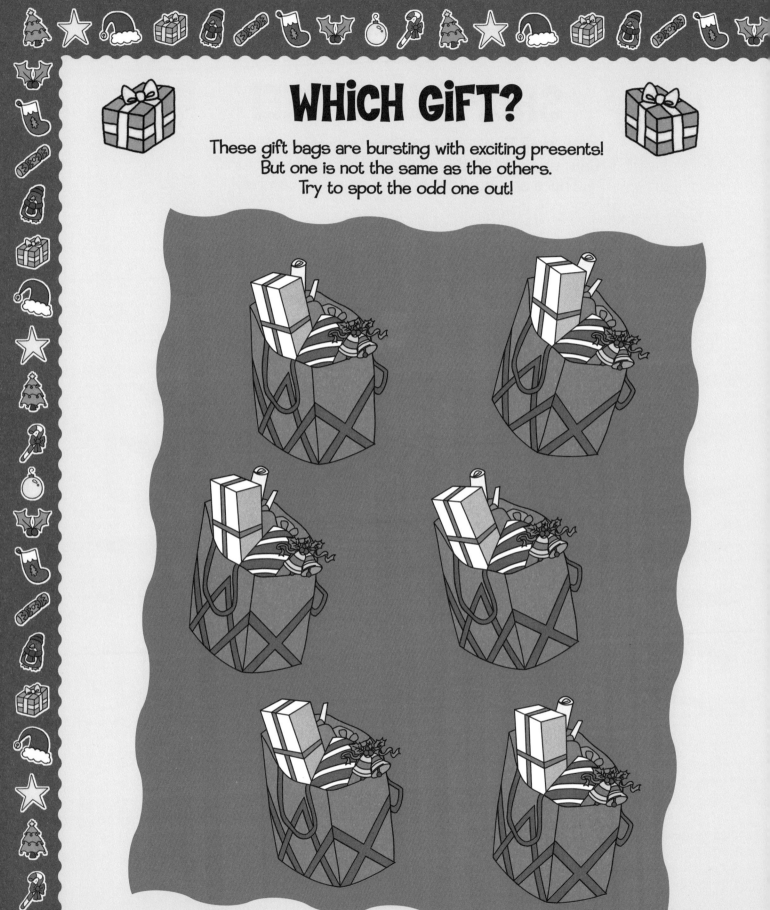

CHOCOLATE GIFTS!

Add a personal touch to your gifts by giving your friends specially wrapped handmade chocolates. Yum!

Here's what you will need

★ 200G (8OZ) FINELY CHOPPED DARK CHOCOLATE ★ 125G (5OZ) WHIPPING CREAM
★ A FEW TABLESPOONS OF COCOA POWDER

Here's how to do it

1 Pour the whipping cream into a heavy saucepan and wait for it to boil.* When it does, remove from the heat and pour into a mixing bowl.

4 When the mixture has cooled and is hard to the touch, scoop out a small amount of chocolate using a teaspoon. Use your hands to shape it into a small ball.

2 Beat the chocolate into the cream using a whisk or electric blender. Beat until the mixture is smooth and all chocolate has melted.

5 Roll the balls into a bowl of cocoa powder, covering them evenly. Place on a plate when done.

3 Chill in the fridge until firm for about 1-3 hours.

6 When all the chocolates are made, wrap them in colourful cellophane or plastic bags and tie with ribbons. Your chocolates are now ready to be given away. Remember to keep them in the fridge, though!

* Ask an adult to help you with this

WATCH THE WORDS!

How good are you at guessing Christmas words?
Unscramble the letters using the picture clues to help you,
and then fill the words in!

1. RATS

_ _ _ _

2. DANCY ACNE

_ _ _ _ _   _ _ _ _

3. PHUDROL

_ _ _ _ _ _ _

4. LYLOH

_ _ _ _ _

5. YIV

_ _ _

iT'S A WRAP!

When you add a creative touch to gift wrapping it becomes even more special. Follow these simple instructions for tips on how to make your presents amazing!

Here's what you will need

★ GIFT IN A BOX ★ CHRISTMAS WRAPPING PAPER ★ STICKY TAPE ★ GLUE
★ SCISSORS ★ PENCIL ★ COLOURED PAPER ★ WHITE PAPER

 Here's how to do it

1  Wrap your gift box with the Christmas wrapping paper.

2 Cut long strips of coloured and white paper about 12cm (4.5 inches) wide. Fold each strip in half lengthways.

3 Along the long folded side, cut two-thirds of the way to the edge of the paper with scissors. Repeat this along the length of the paper.

4  Wind the strips tightly around a pencil. Tape the ends together and remove the pencil.

5 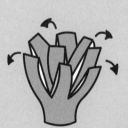 Open up the loops of paper to make a flower.

6 Glue the flowers in bunches on the wrapped present and give it away!

SMART SACK!

Santa's sack has lots of different shapes in it.
Can you spot a shape that appears only once in one colour?

THREE WISE MEN!

Look carefully at the order of the three wise men.
Can you find them in exactly the same order in the box? Search
from left to right, top to bottom and from the bottom upwards!

PARTY PEOPLE!

Here are two identical pictures of a
Christmas family party... or are they? There are six
differences between the two. Can you spot them all?

IT'S IN THE FAMILY!

Look at the words all to do with families. Find them
all inside the family portrait hanging on the wall!

					D	N	A	M	N	I
M	O	T	H	E	R	Y	R	A	N	R	A	T
O	R	I	R	M	G	R	A	N	D	M	A	R
F	A	M	I	L	Y	G	R	E	R	T	R	A
M	R	B	G	U	G	A	U	N	T	M	F	R
I	A	R	A	N	R	M	R	M	R	H	A	U
R	O	R	C	O	U	S	I	N	R	T	D
L	T	U	L	M	F	D	N	R	D	H	E
R	H	O	E	S	L	S	I	S	T	E	R	P
N	E	M	N	P	S	D	F	M	R	R	S
G	R	A	N	D	P	A					

★ Mother   ★ Aunt   ★ Brother
★ Father   ★ Uncle   ★ Sister
★ Grandpa   ★ Cousin   ★ Family
★ Grandma

KNIT KNOTS!

Match the mittens with the jumper to make a perfect set! You can do so by correctly travelling through this maze.

WHO'S THERE?

What does the coded message below tell you about the identity of the lost reindeer? Use the grid to write down each letter carefully to find out!

	1	2	3	4	5
A	E	L	D	P	R
B	T	R	H	U	I
C	O	S	N	E	H

A5 B4 A3 C1 A2 A4 C5   B1 B3 C4

B2 A1 A3   C3 C1 C2 A1 A3

B2 C4 B5 C3 A3 C4 A1 B2!

JINGLE ALL THE WAY!

Santa is off on his way! Use paint, pencils or crayons to colour in the picture using the number key as a guide. Start colouring to see how lovely the Christmas night is!

1 - Red

2 - Light Brown

3 - Light Blue

4 - Orange

5 - Dark Blue

6 - Light Yellow

7 - Dark Brown

8 - Light Green

PiGGYBACK SACK!

Find out how Santa feels carrying that heavy sack of presents! Play this game and see who makes the best team on piggyback.

Number of Players FOUR OR MORE (EVEN NUMBER)
PLUS AN ADULT TO SUPERVISE THE GAME

Materials Required ★ SANTA HATS ★ STONES OR STICK FOR MARKING START/
TURNING LINES ★ A WHISTLE (OPTIONAL)

Object of the Game TO CARRY YOUR PARTNER ON YOUR BACK, SWAP OVER, THEN
RACE BACK TO THE FINISH LINE AS A PAIR.

1 Find a safe area to play in, either on grass or soft sand. Using a stone or a stick, mark out the start and turning lines about 10 metres (30 feet) apart.

2 Divide everyone into pairs.

3 One player in each pair puts on the Santa hat. Their partner lines up in position along the starting line. These players will be Santa's sack.

4 When the supervising adult calls out 'on your marks, get set, go!' or signals the start by blowing a whistle, climb up onto your partner's back (who has the Santa hat on). Loosely wrap your arms around his or her shoulders. Leave your legs dangling by their waist.

Children under the age of 7 should not carry their friends on piggyback! Older children may carry younger ones, though.

5 Your partner holds onto your legs and carries you piggyback towards the turning line. When he or she sets you down, you swap over. This time, you are Santa and your partner is Santa's sack!

6 Race back to the starting line as a pair. The first pair to cross the finish line is the winner!

ALL WRAPPED UP!

Here are two identical pictures of a family wrapping their Christmas presents... or are they? There are six differences between the two. Can you spot them all?

CHRISTMAS CAROLS!

Look carefully at the picture then try answering the questions on the next page. The sharper your memory is, the more answers you will have. Don't be tempted to turn the page for a quick peek!

QUESTIONS

1. How many street lamps do you see?

2. What are the women doing?

3. Which animal is on the street?

4. What will the women collect money in?

5. What is the time?

6. Are there balloons in the shop window?

7. Who is wearing a green and yellow scarf?

8. What are the women holding?

BEAR BUNDLE!

The toy shop has got into a bit of a mess!
Can you count all the bears in this picture?
There are lots that overlap so count carefully!

WHICH TREE IS IT?

Look at these Christmas trees. But one is not the same as the others. Try to spot the odd one out!

CINNAMON BISCUITS!

Add an extra flavour of happiness and cheer with cinnamon biscuits. Keep some for Santa, too!

Here's what you will need

★ 200G (8OZ) FLOUR ★ 1 TEASPOON BAKING POWDER ★ PINCH OF SALT
★ 200ML (7.5 FL OZ) MILK ★ 50G (2OZ) SUGAR ★ 1 TEASPOON CINNAMON
★ 50G (2OZ) MELTED OR VERY SOFT BUTTER
FOR THE GLAZE: 100G (4OZ) ICING SUGAR ★ 2 TABLESPOONS HOT MILK ★ 1/4 TEASPOON VANILLA ESSENCE

Here's how to do it

1

Preheat the oven to 220°C /425°F, or gas mark 7.* Combine the flour, baking powder and salt in a large mixing bowl. Add the milk gradually, stirring with a wooden spoon until you form a soft dough.

2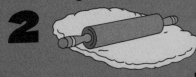

Roll out the dough on a lightly floured surface. Make a 1-cm (1/4-inch) thick rectangle and spread a small amount of melted butter on top.

3 Mix the cinnamon and sugar together in a bowl, then sprinkle evenly over the dough. Then roll up the dough like a swiss roll, starting on the long side.

* Ask an adult to help you with this

4

When the dough is shaped like a log, cut it into 2-cm (1/2-inch) thick slices. Place the slices on a lightly buttered baking tray.

5 Bake in the oven for 18-20 minutes or until golden brown. While they are baking, combine the glaze ingredients in a bowl and beat until you get a smooth paste.

6 Remove the biscuits from the oven* and drizzle with glaze. Serve warm.

WHO AM i?

How good are you at guessing Christmas words?
Unscramble the letters using the picture clues to
help you, and then fill the words in!

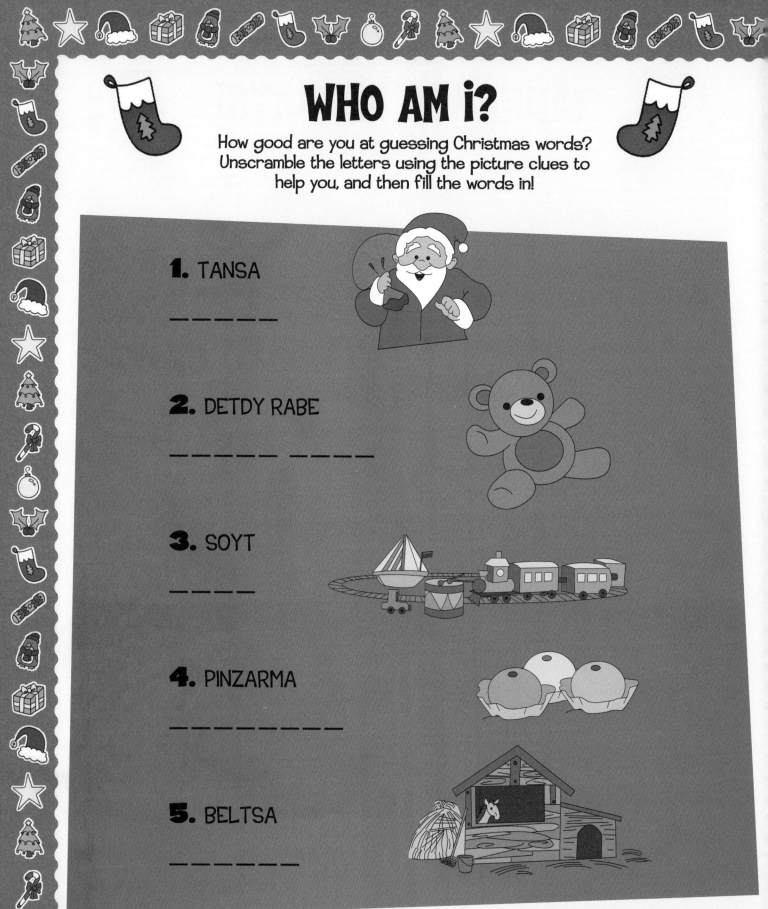

1. TANSA

_ _ _ _ _

2. DETDY RABE

_ _ _ _ _ _ _ _ _

3. SOYT

_ _ _ _

4. PINZARMA

_ _ _ _ _ _ _ _

5. BELTSA

_ _ _ _ _ _

LET THERE BE LIGHT!

Brighten up those dark wintry nights by making a bright and cheerful latern! It's easy to make, so follow these simple instructions and hang this decoration anywhere you want.

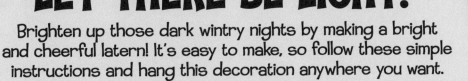

Here's what you will need

★ SHEET OF COLOURED OR DECORATIVE PAPER ★ RULER ★ PENCIL
★ SCISSORS ★ GLUE

Here's how to do it

1 Take a sheet of coloured or patterned paper and draw a line 1 cm from the long edge and 2 cm from the short edge. Cut along the short line. This piece will be used to make the handle.

CUT HERE
1 CM

2  Fold the paper in half lengthways. Along the folded edge measure 1.5 cm sections and cut lines up to the pencil line. Do this along the length of the paper.

3  Unfold the paper and glue the short edges together to form a tube.

4  Glue the handle to the inside of the lantern.

5 Hang your lantern on the Christmas tree or in a window where it catches the light.

TREE TIME!

This Christmas tree has lots of different shapes in it. Can you spot a shape that appears only once in one colour?

NAUGHTY ELVES!

Look carefully at the order of these three naughty elves.
Can you find them in exactly the same order in the box? Search
from left to right, top to bottom and from the bottom upwards!

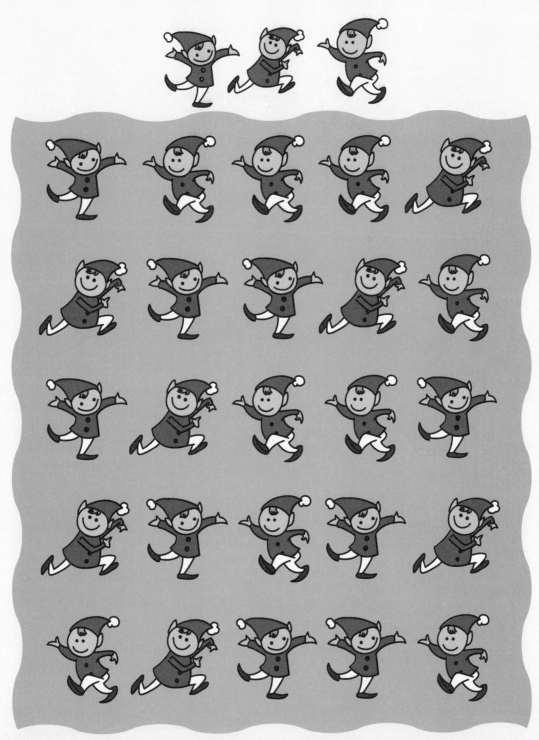

JINGLE BELLS!

Here are two identical pictures of some Christmas decorations... or are they? There are six differences between the two. Can you spot them all?

WHO'S WHO?

Look at the list of seasonal names and
then find them in the puzzle.

G	C	N	I	C	H	O	L	A	S
A	W	T	U	M	N	T	P	I	Y
B	M	D	M	A	D	O	N	N	A
R	A	T	G	M	Q	U	X	I	Z
I	R	H	U	M	J	E	S	U	S
E	Y	Q	I	M	O	G	F	J	U
L	P	S	U	M	S	O	P	K	Y
R	A	T	N	O	E	L	R	L	D
R	B	N	V	O	P	D	P	M	A
F	A	E	W	M	H	C	B	N	V
R	O	T	X	M	H	O	E	Y	I
E	M	M	A	N	U	E	L	Z	D
Q	A	T	U	M	N	O	P	A	Y

★ Mary   ★ Gabriel   ★ Noel

★ Nicholas   ★ David   ★ Emmanuel

★ Joseph   ★ Jesus   ★ Madonna

ELF HELP!

Poor elf! Santa's little helper has lost his way to the toy workshop. Help him reach it by taking the right path through this maze.

COLOURFUL CAROLS!

We all love singing carols! But it's much more fun when there is a bit of colour around. Use paint, pencils or crayons to colour in the picture using the number key as a guide.

1 - Red

2 - Black

3 - Brown

4 - Pink

5 - Yellow

6 - Blue

7 - Orange

8 - Green

CHAIN REACTION!

How well can you mime and explain
something through actions rather than words?
Find out by playing this game with your friends!

Number of Players FIVE OR MORE.

Materials Required NONE.

Object of the Game TO WORK OUT WHAT THE FIRST PLAYER WAS THINKING OF.

1 All players stand in a line. Players 1 and 2 face each other and the other players close their eyes.

2 The first person in line mimes something typical of the Christmas season to the second person. This could be Santa sliding down the chimney, decorating the tree, or the reindeer pulling the sleigh!

3 Then the first person says 'OK' and turns to the front. The third person opens their eyes and the second person repeats the mime, to the third player. This process of imitation is repeated until it is the turn of the last player in the line.

4 The last person has to guess what the first player in line was trying to communicate. The person who has just made a guess then moves to the top of the line and performs a new mime. This game is guaranteed to be very funny!

A BUSY STREET!

Look carefully at the picture then try answering the questions on the next page. The sharper your memory is, the more answers you will have. Don't be tempted to turn the page for a quick peek!

QUESTIONS

1. How many snowmen can you see?

2. What is the little boy playing with?

3. Is there a star on the Chrismas tree?

4. How many dummies are there in the shop windows?

5. Are all the children wearing hats?

6. Is it snowing?

7. How many children are there?

8. What animal is in the picture?

BOW WOW!

It's time to start wrapping those presents! But do you have enough bows? You'll have to count them all. There are lots that overlap so count carefully!

Look at these little boys having fun in the snow.
But one is not the same as the others. Try to spot
the odd one out!

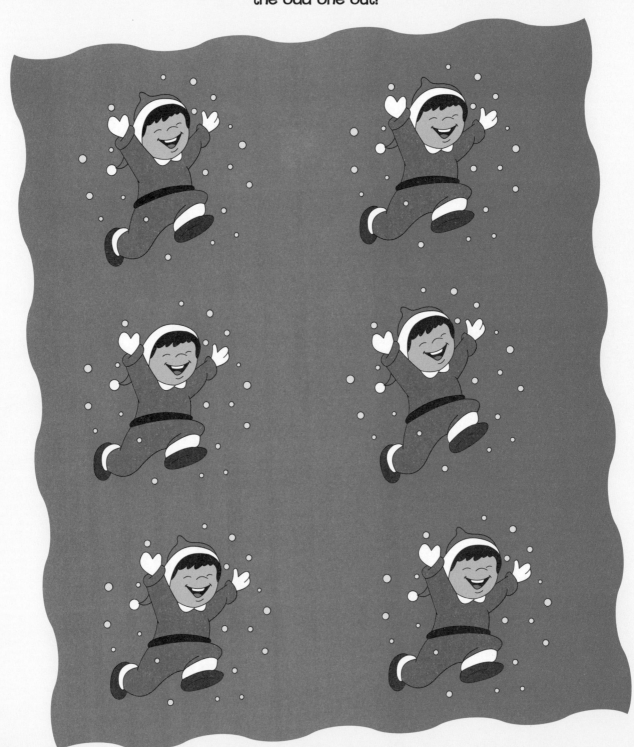

MAGIC MINCE PIES!

It's just not Christmas without mince pies! Try your hand at these to score top marks with your friends and family.

Here's what you will need

★ 100G (4OZ) SOFTENED BUTTER ★ 200G (8OZ) PLAIN FLOUR
★ 25G (1OZ) CASTER SUGAR ★ 200G (8OZ) MINCEMEAT (FROM A JAR)
★ 1 EGG YOLK ★ A FEW TABLESPOONS OF COLD WATER ★ 1 BEATEN EGG

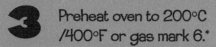 ## Here's how to do it

1 Sieve the flour into the mixing bowl and then add the butter. Using your fingertips, rub the butter into the flour until it looks like breadcrumbs. Make sure your hands are clean!

2  Stir in the sugar, egg yolk and about 3-4 tablespoons of cold water to make a soft dough. Wrap the dough in cling film and chill in the fridge for 30 minutes.

3 Preheat oven to 200°C /400°F or gas mark 6.*

4 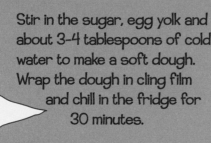 Roll out the dough on a floured surface and cut 15 circles using a round pastry cutter. Cut another 15 using a slightly smaller round cutter.

* Ask an adult to help you with this

5 Grease the bun tins lightly with butter and line them with the larger circles. Heap  on a teaspoon of mincemeat. Dampen the edges of the smaller rounds with a little water and lay them over the mincemeat to form lids. Prick the top of the pies with a fork and make sure the edges are tightly sealed.

6 Brush the tops with beaten egg and bake in the oven for 25-30 minutes until golden brown. Remove from the oven* and cool on a wire tray. Eat them while they're still warm!

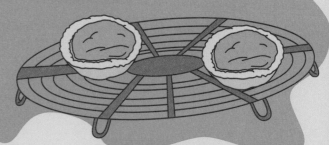

PICTURE CLUES!

How good are you at guessing Christmas words?
Unscramble the letters using the picture clues to help
you, and then fill the words in!

1. YONKED

_ _ _ _ _ _

2. WOB

_ _ _

3. FUMERFAS

_ _ _ _ _ _ _ _

4. LUYE GOL

_ _ _ _ _ _ _

SUPER STOCKING!

Make your own special stocking this Christmas eve. All you will need to impress Santa are some simple supplies and some inspiration!

Here's what you will need:

★ COLOURED FELT ★ COLOURED THREAD OR RIBBON ★ SCISSORS
★ GLUE ★ A HOLE PUNCH ★ GLITTER AND DECORATIVE SHAPES ★ A MARKER PEN

  ## Here's how to do it

1  Take the coloured felt and fold it in half. Draw a large stocking shape on it with the marker pen. Cut along the shape to get two stocking pieces.

4  Take the thread or ribbon and weave it in and out of the holes. Leave a loop of thread at one end and tie it in a knot. Now you can hang it up!

2  Glue the two stockings together around the edges. Take care to keep the top open. Don't glue it shut or you won't get any presents!

5 Decorate your stocking with glitter and Christmas pictures. Your super stocking is ready to impress Santa!

3  Punch holes all around the edges of the stocking (but not at the top).

BAUBLE BREAK!

This shiny bauble has lots of different shapes in it.
Can you spot a shape that appears only once in one colour?

TREE TEST!

Look carefully at the order of these Christmas trees. Can you find them in exactly the same order in the box? Search from left to right, top to bottom and from the bottom upwards!

A BIG TOY SACK!

Here are two identical pictures of Santa with his sack of toys... or are they? There are six differences between the two. Can you spot them all?

HOLIDAY CHEER!

There's so much fun to be had over the Christmas holidays! Look at the list of fun words and find them in the holly wreath.

★ Celebrations

★ Charity

★ Decoration

★ Shopping

★ Holidays

★ Sharing

★ Cheer

STOP HIM!

The gingerbread man is running away!
Help the old woman catch him by finding the
right path through this maze.

CHRISTMAS CHAOS!

Here are some words all to do with Christmas that have got jumbled up! Can you unscramble the letters and rearrange them into words?

1. E L E C B A I R O T N S

_ _ _ _ _ _ _ _ _ _ _

2. Y K T E U R

_ _ _ _ _ _

3. A S F E T

_ _ _ _ _

4. O M C E T

_ _ _ _ _

5. L I G E T T R

_ _ _ _ _ _ _

CHRISTMAS EVE!

The night before Christmas is always the most exciting time of the season! Use paint, pencils or crayons to colour in the picture using the number key as a guide.

1 - Red

2 - Yellow

3 - Green

4 - Blue

5 - Light Blue

6 - Light Brown

7 - Dark Brown

8 - Black

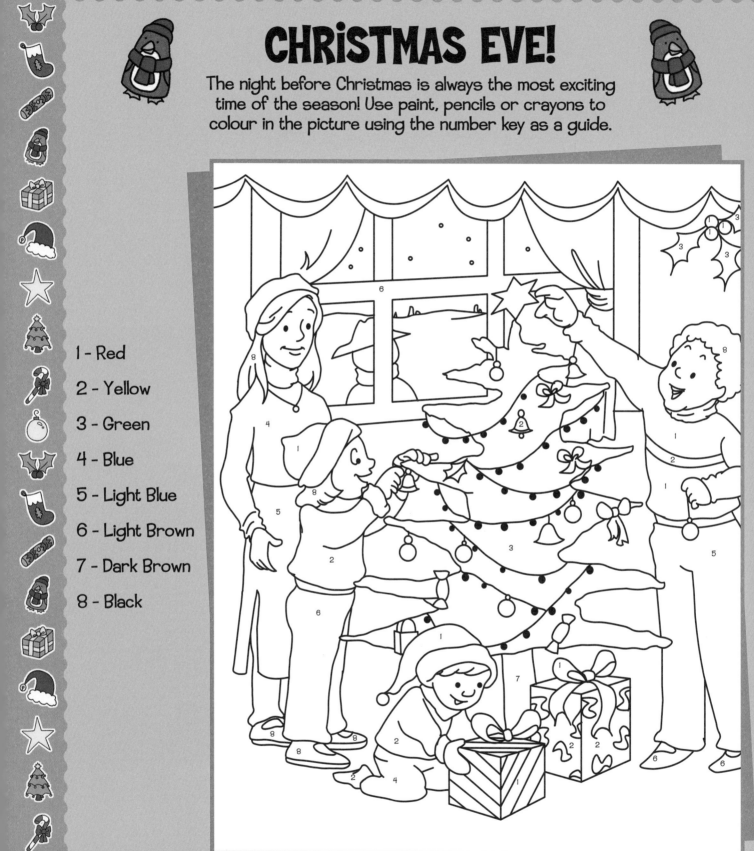

CAROL CLUES!

How well do you know your Christmas carols?
Play this fun game with your friends to find out!

Number of Players FOUR OR MORE

Materials Required NONE

Object of the Game TO GUESS THE CAROL AFTER HEARING JUST A FEW NOTES.

1 Choose a player to be the hummer. If you are this person, start the game by humming or whistling the first note of a carol.

2 The other players try to guess the name of the song from that single note. Players take it in turns trying to guess the Christmas tune. You'll see just how tricky it is to do!

3 Now repeat the beginning of the melody, adding one note each time until someone finally guesses the carol.

4 This person is the winner and becomes the hummer in the next round! To make it even more fun you could play for sweets or other treats.

BAUBLE BEAUTY!

Would you like to make some baubles for the Christmas tree? They are really easy to make. All you need to do is follow these simple instructions and you'll soon have some to hang on the tree!

Here's what you will need

★ ROUND, CLEAR PLASTIC FOOD CONTAINER LID ★ GLUE ★ OLD NEWSPAPER
★ GLITTER AND SEQUINS IN DIFFERENT COLOURS ★ TINSEL ★ A HOLE PUNCH ★ A PAINTBRUSH

Here's how to do it

1 Cover the table with sheets of old newspaper to protect it.

2 Place the different glitters and sequins into separate dishes or bowls and pour some glue in a container (an old yoghurt pot is ideal).

3  Take a clear plastic lid and wipe it clean. Use a paintbrush to apply glue on the outer side of the lid.

4  Sprinkle the glitter and sequins on to the lid. You can either use the glitter in a design you have in mind or simply make pretty patterns.

5 When dry, repeat the process with the other side. The glue will dry clear leaving the round lid bright and sparkly.

6 Use a holepunch to make a hole at the top of the lid and thread it with a piece of tinsel.

7 Your bauble is finished! Hang it in front of a window or near a light so that the glitter and sequins can sparkle!

TREE FUN!

Look carefully at the picture then try answering questions on the next page. The sharper your memory is, the more answers you will have. Don't be tempted to turn the page for a quick peek!

 # QUESTIONS

1. How many ribbons are lying on the floor?

2. What is the girl picking up?

3. Is there a dog in the picture?

4. What is the mother putting on the tree?

5. What is the older girl standing on?

6. Is the boy wearing a hat?

7. Who is wearing a scarf?

8. How many stars are there on the tree?

EQUAL ELVES!

These little elves are all busy making toys. But one is not the quite same as the others! Try to spot the odd one out.

PARTY HATS!

Forget paper hats from the crackers - make your own fun, bright and cheery hats to really get the party swinging!

Here's what you will need

★ SQUARE OF COLOURED OR DECORATIVE PAPER ★ STICKY TAPE ★ RULER
★ PENCIL ★ GLITTER ★ SEQUINS ★ GLUE ★ FELT-TIP PENS

Here's how to do it

1 Fold the coloured paper exactly in half from top to bottom.

2 Fold the sheet in half again - from left to right - to make a crease then unfold the paper to leave just the first fold.

3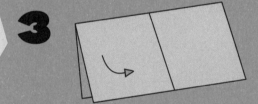

Hold the paper with the folded edge at the top and the open end at the bottom. Fold the top left corner down to the bottom.

4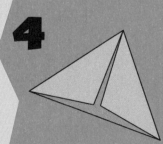

Fold the right corner down in the same way to make a triangle.

5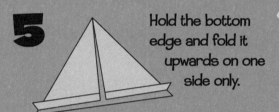

Hold the bottom edge and fold it upwards on one side only.

6 Turn the triangle over and fold the other bottom edge upwards to form the hat brim. You may want to use some glue or tape to hold it in position.

7 Decorate your hat with felt-tip pens, glitter and sequins. You can make it as colourful and decorative as you want... then make more for everyone else!

BOW BITS!

This big bow has lots of different shapes in it.
Can you spot a shape that appears only once in one colour?

CANDLE CLUES!

Look carefully at the order of the three shining candles below.
Can you find them in exactly the same order in the box? Search from
left to right, top to bottom and from the bottom upwards!

FAULTY FLIGHT!

Here are two identical pictures of Santa flying in his sleigh...
or are they? There are six differences between the two.
Can you spot them all?

REINDEER RUCKUS!

Look at the names of all of Santa's reindeer helpers.
There are lots of them! Find them all in the puzzle.

★ Rudolph ★ Dancer ★ Blitzen
★ Comet ★ Prancer ★ Vixen
★ Cupid ★ Donner ★ Dasher

	V	I	X	E	N			
C	P	C	R	D	C	D	D	C
D	R	C	U	P	I	D	A	C
O	A	C	D	R	A	C	S	D
C	N	N	R	O	R	A	C	H	C
D	N	C	B	L	I	T	Z	E	N
C	E	E	O	P	R	A	C	R	C
R	R	R	C	H	R	A	C	S	D
D	A	N	C	E	R	S		
C	D	R	A	C	S			
C	O	M	E	T	S			
D	R	A	C					

HELP SANTA!

Have you been good this year?
This boy has! Help Santa reach his house by
finding the path through this maze.

GIFT GALLERY!

Let's make Christmas colourful! Use paint, pencils or crayons to colour in the picture using the number key as a guide.

1 – Red

2 – Yellow

3 – Light Blue

4 – Purple

5 – Pink

6 – Dark Blue

7 – Green

8 – Light Brown

9 – Dark Brown

10 – Orange

SANTA SAYS!

You'd better do what Santa says or
you won't get any presents!

Number of Players THREE OR MORE

Materials Required A COIN

Object of the Game TO COPY THE ACTIONS OF THE PLAYER WHO IS
SANTA. HE OR SHE MUST SAY 'SANTA SAYS...' EVERY TIME AN INSTRUCTION IS
GIVEN TO THE OTHER PLAYERS.

1 Toss a coin to choose who
will be Santa.

2 The other players stand in a line
facing this person.

3 If you are Santa, begin the game
by giving the group instructions
they can follow. Remember to always
start any command with the words
'Santa says...' For example, 'Santa
says clap your hands!' or 'Santa
says jump up and down!' Everyone
copies your movements and tries
not to make any mistakes.

4 The person playing Santa then
starts to mix in instructions that
don't start with 'Santa says',
for example, 'Clap your hands.'
Players don't follow instructions
unless the command begins with
'Santa says...'

5 Players drop out one by one as
they make a mistake until there is
one person left in the game. This
person is Santa in the next round!

Did you know that this game began
as an army drill?

GINGER ZING!

Here are six tasty and festive-looking gingerbread men. But one is not the same as the others. Try to spot the odd one out!

CHRISTMAS PARTY!

Look carefully at the picture then try answering the questions on the next page. The sharper your memory is, the more answers you will have. Don't be tempted to turn the page for a quick peek!

QUESTIONS

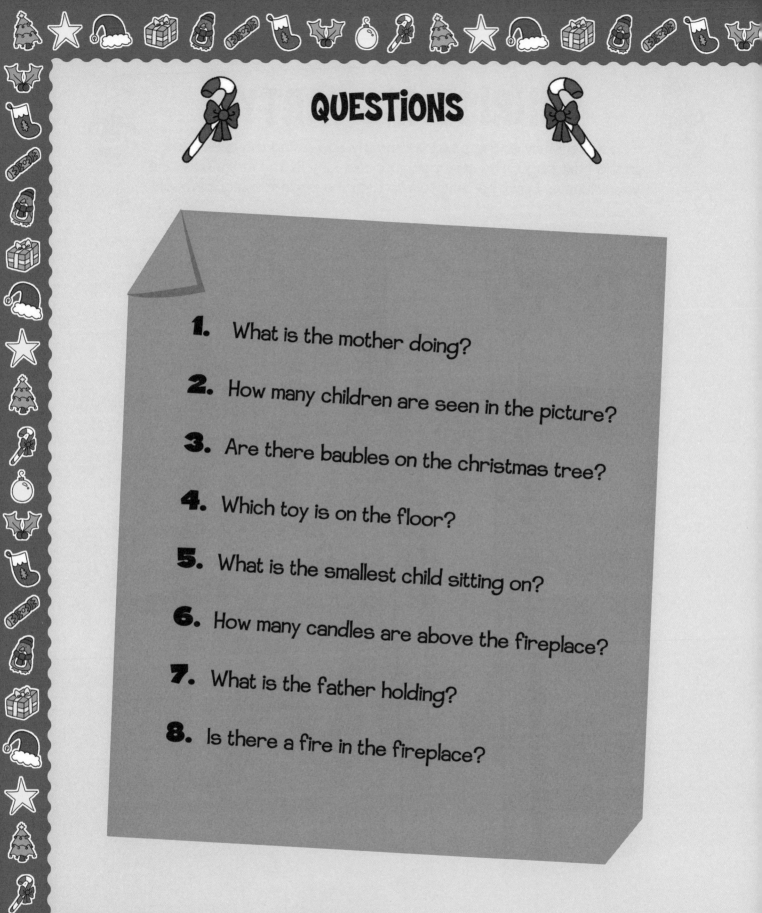

1. What is the mother doing?

2. How many children are seen in the picture?

3. Are there baubles on the christmas tree?

4. Which toy is on the floor?

5. What is the smallest child sitting on?

6. How many candles are above the fireplace?

7. What is the father holding?

8. Is there a fire in the fireplace?

TRICKY TREES!

These Christmas trees are all standing close together.
Can you count how many there are in this picture?
Lots of them overlap so make sure you count carefully!

WHAT'S THE WORD?

How good are you at guessing Christmas words?
Unscramble the letters using the picture clues to help
you, and then fill the words in!

1. BIBRON

_ _ _ _ _ _

2. RISEREB

_ _ _ _ _ _ _

3. DRAC

_ _ _ _

4. SEWI NEM

_ _ _ _ _ _

5. ANTNERL

_ _ _ _ _ _ _

DEAR REINDEER!

Send Rudolph to a friend! Follow these simple instructions and make a Rudolph card to share your Christmas greetings.

Here's what you will need

★ PLAIN WHITE CARD ★ BLUE CARD OR PAPER ★ BROWN PAPER
★ SMALL BLACK BEADS ★ COTTON WOOL BALLS ★ A TINY BELL ★ SCISSORS
★ A BLACK MARKER PEN ★ RIBBON ★ GLUE ★ RED AND BROWN FELT-TIP PENS

 ## Here's how to do it

1 Take the white card and cover top half of front side with the blue card or paper.

2  Now draw the shape of a reindeer on the brown paper and cut along the drawing. Cut it out and glue it to the card.

3 Use two black beads for Rudolph's eyes, and a cotton wool ball for his nose. Glue them in place and colour in the cotton wool nose with the felt-tip pens. Add hooves and antler details with the black marker.

4  As a special finishing touch, attach the tiny bell to a small piece of a ribbon and glue it around Rudolph's neck.

5 Your Rudolph card is ready. And what's more, it makes a festive tinkling sound too!

SNOWMAN SPOTTER!

These snowmen have all been made the same. But one is not the quite same as the others! Try to spot the odd one out.

DOWN THE CHIMNEY!
This chimney has lots of different shapes on it.
Can you spot a shape that appears only once in one colour?

CONE SEQUENCE!

Look carefully at the order of the three pine cones below.
Can you find them in exactly the same order in the box? Search from
left to right, top to bottom and from the bottom upwards!

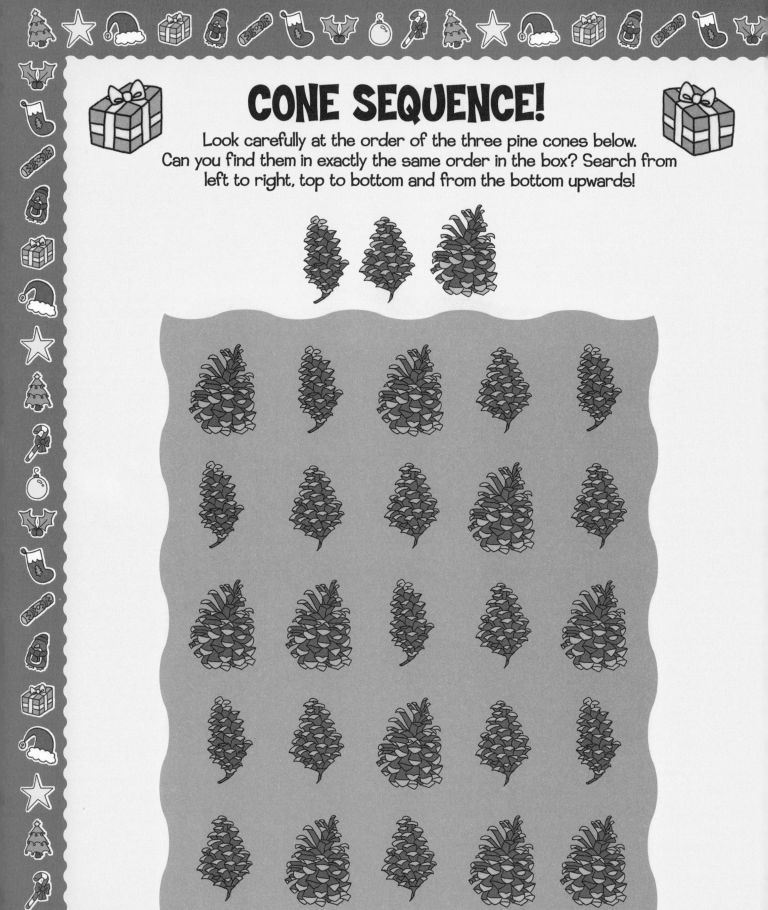

ANSWERS

PAGE 6

PAGE 7

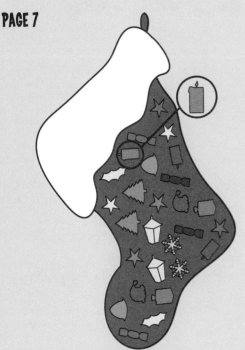

PAGE 9

1. BAUBLE
2. FEAST
3. SCARF
4. SHEPHERD
5. SLEIGH

PAGE 11

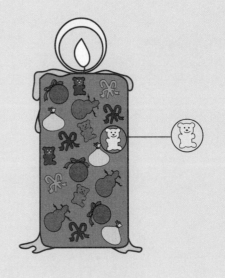

PAGE 12

ANSWERS

PAGE 13

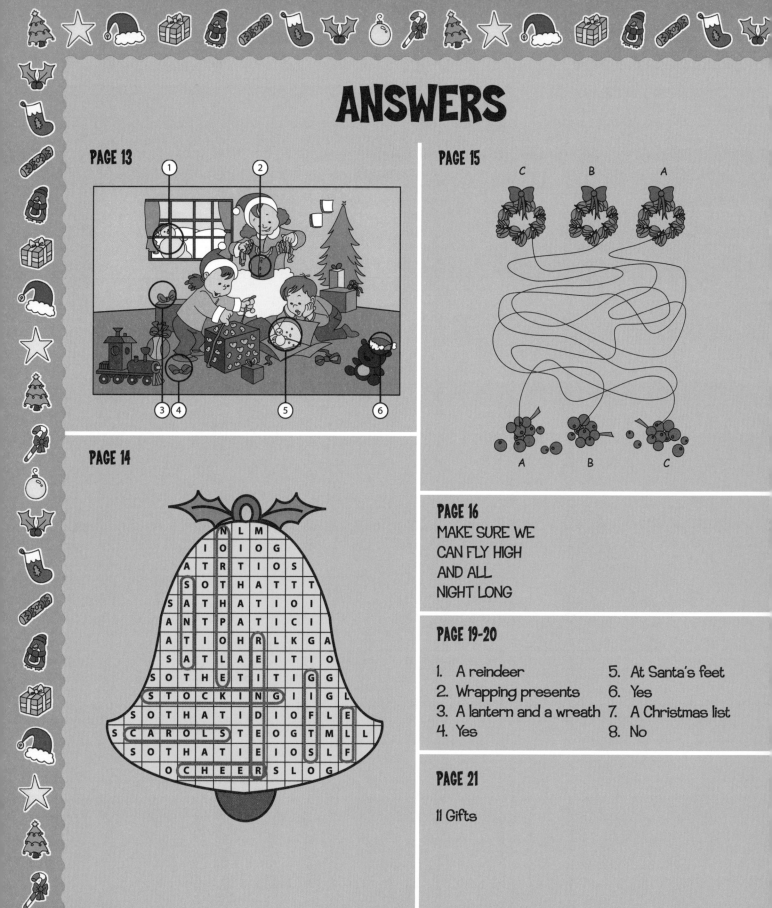

PAGE 14

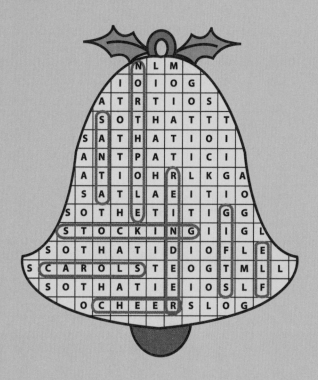

PAGE 15

PAGE 16
MAKE SURE WE
CAN FLY HIGH
AND ALL
NIGHT LONG

PAGE 19-20

1. A reindeer
2. Wrapping presents
3. A lantern and a wreath
4. Yes

5. At Santa's feet
6. Yes
7. A Christmas list
8. No

PAGE 21

11 Gifts

ANSWERS

PAGE 22

PAGE 24

1. SNOWFLAKE
2. FIREPLACE
3. MANGER
4. NATIVITY
5. LIGHTS

PAGE 26

PAGE 27

PAGE 28

ANSWERS

PAGE 29

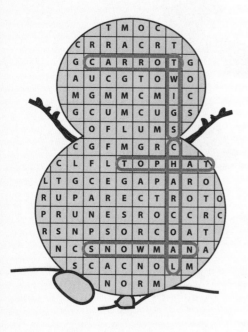

PAGE 30

PAGE 31

CHRISTMAS TREE
DECORATIONS
ELVES
DECEMBER
PRANCER

PAGE 34

PAGE 35-36

1. 2
2. Yes
3. Yes
4. A dog
5. A hat
6. A house
7. 4
8. 1

PAGE 37

15 Stockings

ANSWERS

PAGE 38

PAGE 42

PAGE 40

1. MINCE PIE
2. CHURCH
3. PUDDING
4. GIFT
5. CAROL

PAGE 43

PAGE 44

ANSWERS

PAGE 45

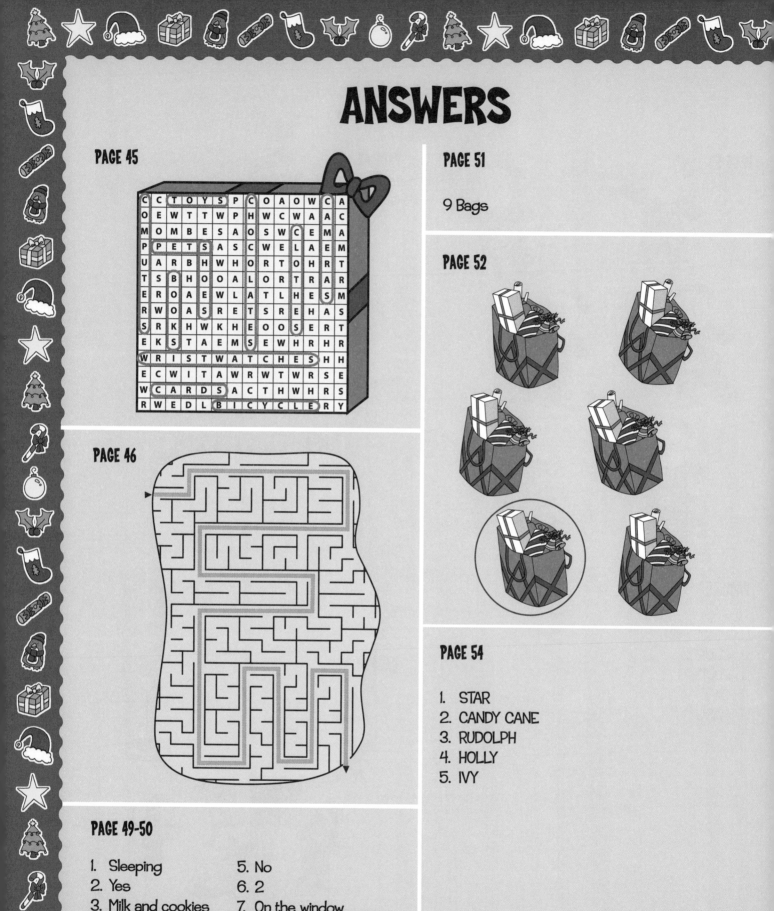

PAGE 46

PAGE 49-50

1. Sleeping
2. Yes
3. Milk and cookies
4. 15
5. No
6. 2
7. On the window
8. 1

PAGE 51

9 Bags

PAGE 52

PAGE 54

1. STAR
2. CANDY CANE
3. RUDOLPH
4. HOLLY
5. IVY

120

ANSWERS

PAGE 56

PAGE 58

PAGE 57

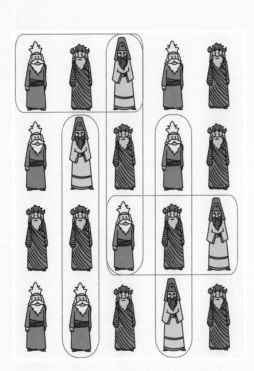

PAGE 59

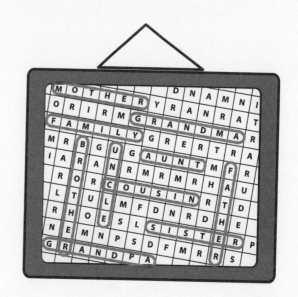

ANSWERS

PAGE 60

PAGE 61

RUDOLPH THE RED NOSED REINDEER!

PAGE 64

PAGE 65-66

1. 2
2. Singing carols
3. A horse
4. A hat
5. 12 o'clock
6. Yes
7. The woman in the centre
8. A book

PAGE 67

10 Bears

PAGE 68

ANSWERS

PAGE 70

1. SANTA
2. TEDDY BEAR
3. TOYS
4. MARZIPAN
5. STABLE

PAGE 72

PAGE 73

PAGE 74

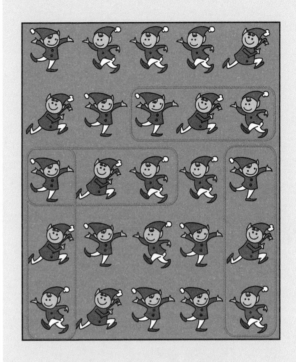

ANSWERS

PAGE 75

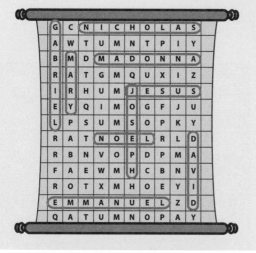

PAGE 76

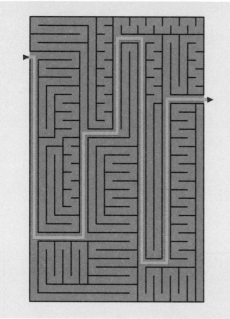

PAGE 79-80

1. 2
2. A ball
3. Yes
4. 2
5. No
6. No
7. 5
8. A dog

PAGE 81

11 Bows

PAGE 82

PAGE 84

1. DONKEY
2. BOW
3. EARMUFFS
4. YULE LOG

ANSWERS

PAGE 86

PAGE 88

PAGE 87

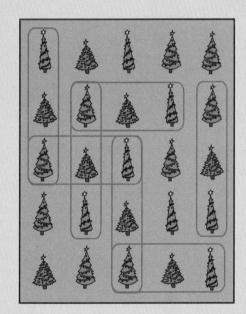

PAGE 89

ANSWERS

PAGE 90

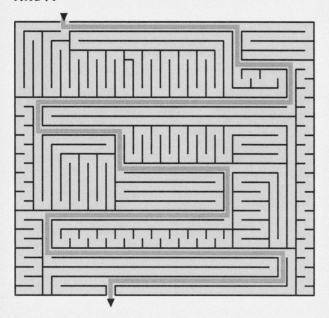

PAGE 91

CELEBRATIONS
TURKEY
FEAST
COMET
GLITTER

PAGE 95-96

1. 2
2. A stocking
3. No
4. A stocking
5. A stool
6. No
7. The mother
8. 4

PAGE 97

PAGE 99

PAGE 100

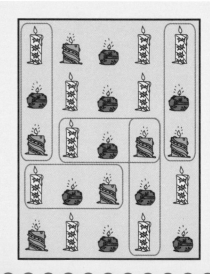

ANSWERS

PAGE 101

PAGE 102

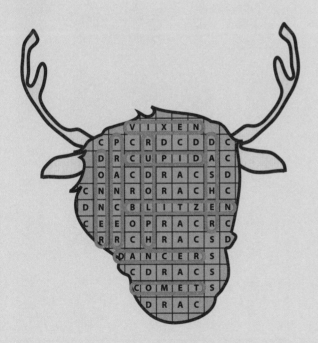

PAGE 103

PAGE 106

PAGE 107-108

1. Hugging a child
2. 5
3. Yes
4. A teddy bear
5. On a rocking horse
6. 2
7. A gift
8. No

ANSWERS

PAGE 109

8 Trees

PAGE 110

1. RIBBON
2. BERRIES
3. CARD
4. WISE MEN
5. LANTERN

PAGE 112

PAGE 113

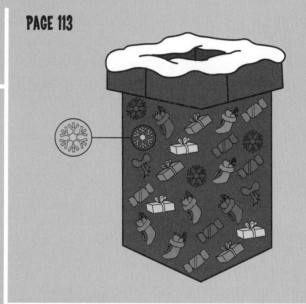

PAGE 114

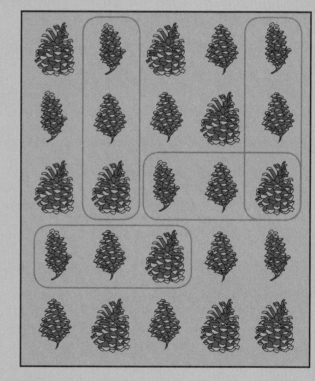